Quotable
RUDY

Quotable
RUDY

**Words of Insight, Savvy, and Survival
by and about RUDY GIULIANI,
a Mayor for America**

Monte Carpenter

TowleHouse Publishing
Nashville, Tennessee

TowleHouse books are distributed by National Book Network (NBN),
4720 Boston Way, Lanham, Maryland 20706.

Library of Congress Cataloging-in-Publication data is available.
ISBN: 0-931249-16-4

**A portion of the royalties from this book will be donated to the
American Red Cross in memory of the victims of the September 11
terrorist attacks.**

Cover design by Gore Studio, Inc.
Page design by Mike Towle

Printed in the United States of America
1 2 3 4 5 6 — 06 05 04 03 02

CONTENTS

INTRODUCTION

B eing the mayor of New York City is in some respects similar to coaching UCLA basketball, playing James Bond in the movies, or hosting *The Tonight Show*. There's no place to hide; everyone and his uncle has an opinion about your suitability for the job; and a day rarely goes by that you're not measured against the acts, attitudes, and accomplishments of predecessors. Big shoes must be filled, and every move and manner gets scrutinized. Still, being New York City mayor is somewhat more serious than Final Fours, martinis shaken not stirred, and knocking out a nightly monologue.

Rudy Giuliani is one of those special people who elicits either affection or scorn. People either love him or hate him, although the scales have tipped heavily toward the former since the tragic events of September 11, 2001. With Rudy Giuliani, there's no in-between. Giuliani is to Big Apple politics what Howard Cosell was to TV sportscasting, what Notre Dame is to college football, and what Giuliani's beloved New York Yankees are to baseball.

Long before September 11 dawned as a day in infamy, providing a horrible backdrop for Giuliani's instant rise to national hero, the New York City mayor had boldly made his mark on the town. Out with the squeegee operators and panhandlers, in with the get-tough-on-crime action over rhetoric. In large part because of Rudy, New York City returned to its glory days as a popular destination for business travelers and tourists. People could again walk from Times Square to Central Park without feeling compelled to look over their shoulders every two minutes. This had to be a source of pride for the native son.

Giuliani, born to a working-class family in Brooklyn and the grandson of Italian immigrants, served eight years as New York City mayor following a quarter-century of work as an attorney. He was a U.S. associate attorney general for a number of years, and then in 1983 he was appointed U.S. Attorney for the Southern District of New York. He used that position of clout to take down drug dealers and white-collar criminals, and to rid the city of much of its government corruption and organized crime. Ultimately, he earned more than four thousand convictions against only twenty-five reversals. His success in the courtroom translated well to a run for political office. Although Giuliani was narrowly defeated in his first run for mayor in 1989, he came back in 1993 to beat incumbent David Dinkins and take charge as a mayor who would challenge, change, and, at times, even charm the city.

There was little conciliatory about Giuliani's approach to being New York City mayor. Clearly, he basked in the limelight even while his motives seemed to go far beyond winning friends and cultivating a polished image. During Giuliani's two years as New York City mayor, crime was trimmed by 57 percent and murder was reduced 65 percent, in large part explaining why the FBI had touted New York as the safest large city in America five years running. Giuliani did more between 1993 and 2001, however, than take a big bite out of Big Apple crime. He cut city welfare rolls in half while helping more than six hundred thousand individuals find gainful employment and a means to support themselves and their families. He also spearheaded the improvement of the city's public-school system, starting with ending principal tenure and raising the public school system's annual operating budget from $8 million to $12 million, allowing for reformation of programs such as bilingual education and special education and the introduction of innovative reading and computer programs, as well as the restoration of arts education.

The glowing mayoral report tells only that half of the story that we can see and touch on paper. Rudy's real legacy, the one that gets etched in cranial stone, lies in how he handled and reacted to (not so good at times) the events, mishaps, and tragedies of his last two years in office: the announced run for the U.S. Senate against First Lady Hillary Rodham Clinton; the breakup of a marriage amid a well-publicized relationship with another woman; the diagnosis of prostate cancer; the dropping-out of the Senate race; the September 11 terrorist attacks on the World Trade Center, followed just two months later by the numbing crash of American Flight 587 minutes after departing from JFK Airport.

Even before the dust had settled, literally and figuratively, New York City had elected a new mayor, businessman Michael Bloomberg, to succeed Giuliani, whose approval rating had sky-rocketed to unprecedented levels. Giuliani's hands-on work and leadership during the September 11 rescue-and-recovery opera-tions, as well as his galvanizing a city and a nation with crisis-cool compassion, solidified his legacy. It was a succession of moments devoid of politics and infused with leadership instincts set in motion. When Giuliani left office on December 31, 2001, to begin the next phase of his life, higher office seemed likely. Perhaps a run for governor. Maybe, someday, another shot at the U.S. Senate. A spot on President George W. Bush's 2004 reelection ticket, replacing Dick Cheney, has even been men-tioned as a possibility.

Giuliani doesn't mince words, and he's not shy about expressing an opinion. Perhaps he is a Type-A personality. He can be Abrasive; he has an "Attitude"; he Antagonizes and/or Alienates a fair share of people; and he has been known to pop off in Anger. Stepping on toes goes with his territory. Yet he is media savvy. Some reporters might even call him a bully, but in truth they love it: It makes their job easier. Today's journalism really isn't about reporting the news: It's about finding a hook that arouses emotions in readers and viewers, and Giuliani does that.

With Rudy, the plot always thickens. His blunt, oft-unfiltered talk is refreshing in a day and age when champions of civil rights will blast a nonliberal exercise of free speech, in some such cases defending the "rights" of citizens to not be offended. In a society that continues to edge closer to gray, Giuliani stands out as black and white.

Quotable Rudy is a compilation of approximately three hundred of Giuliani's most memorable, cut-to-the-chase quotes. No nonsense; minimal pretense. Hundreds of thousands of his words, gleaned from speeches, ceremonies, press releases, books, newspaper and magazine articles, and his own weekly columns, comprised the ton of clay that was then sculpted, whittled, cut and pasted, and further trimmed to create this bite-sized record of Giuliani's best and brightest insights on a variety of subjects. New York. Politics. Crime. New York's Finest and Bravest. September 11. These and dozens of other hot-button topics are covered. This book offers a Cliff's Notes version of Giuliani's years as mayor and a few blasts from his past, and input from the occasional naysayer as well as yea-sayer. *Quotable Rudy* is Essential Rudy.

Politics as Unusual

The era of fear has had a long enough reign. The period of doubt has run its course.

~

It always appeared to me that the city of New York traditionally did better when the mayor was somewhat unpredictable, when the mayor was not a complete captive of one political party or the other.

~

WE WERE REPUBLICANS AND REFORMERS COMING INTO CITY HALL,
SO IT WASN'T GOING TO BE EASY. WE HAD TO BE TOUGH. EVERYONE
WAS AGAINST US.[1]

*—Peter Powers, a longtime friend of
Giuliani's and deputy mayor in his first term*

HE IS A BULLY. HE USES FEAR AND INTIMIDATION TO ACCOMPLISH
THINGS.[2]

*—David Dinkins, Giuliani's mayoral
predecessor and 1993 mayoral opponent*

If I had his record, I'd be kind of embarrassed to show my face.[3]
—Giuliani about David Dinkins

HE IS ON THE CUSP OF BEING HELD IN VERY LOW REGARD. HE'S HIS
OWN WORST ENEMY. THERE'S NO RESERVOIR OF GOODWILL. WHEN
HE STARTS GOING DOWN THE INCLINE, WHICH IS HAPPENING,
THERE WILL BE NOBODY THERE TO SUPPORT HIM, BECAUSE THEY'LL
ALL BE KICKING HIM. . . . WHY DOES THE SCORPION STING? IT'S THE
NATURE OF A SCORPION.[4]

*—Ed Koch, former New York mayor whose contributions to society since
leaving office include presiding as judge on TV's* The People's Court

He's dying for a corruption scandal in my administration so that he doesn't end up with the most corrupt administration in the last half of the twentieth century.[5]

—*Giuliani on Koch*

⌒

The city is used to politicians who submit to whatever is the safest thing to do. I think the city needs to be broken of that.[6]

—*spoken during his first term as mayor*

⌒

The left-wing elite opposes me because I have shown that a Republican can win elections by wide margins, even in a Democratic stronghold like New York City, with a bold, unapologetic, Ronald Reagan-style conservative agenda.[7]

⌒

There isn't a Democratic or Republican way to run New York. When cities have such complex problems, they need the freedom to select the best solutions.[8]

⌒

I've studied the careers of other politicians, and they start off wanting to achieve things but lose courage. They become placaters of the popular mood instead of having confidence that your ultimate goal is correct and simply moving toward it.[9]

New York is a great intellectual center that has become one of the most backward parts of America—unwilling to think a new thought. I absolutely love, and maybe I overdo this a little, to suggest something new and then watch the reaction to it.[10]

I'm not a partisan operative of the Republican Party. I grew up in an era when Democrats and Republicans used to work with each other.[11]

Politicians in this city really don't help because they have no idea how to deal with private enterprise. They scapegoat business.[12]

I haven't been able to communicate my message to the African American community as well as I should. Maybe it's my own inadequacies.[13]

~

The left-wing elite is pouring everything into this race because they see Mrs. Clinton as their champion. They are also furious that my tough law-and-order, pro-free-enterprise policies have succeeded in making New York City great again.[14]

~

It's funny; I haven't seen her at a Yankees game. I've been at Yankee Stadium maybe a thousand times in my life, and I've yet to see Hillary Clinton there.[15]

—reacting to one-time senatorial campaign rival Hillary Clinton's claim that she had always been a fan of the Yankees

~

From the day that I started exploring running for mayor, I have made it clear to every political leader almost from the first discussion we have had that there will be no jobs or patronage—only decisions made as merit.[16]

~

RUDY GIULIANI WAS NOT HANDSOME, LIKE LINDSAY, OR FUNNY, LIKE KOCH. HE COULDN'T EVEN QUALIFY AS IRASCIBLE, LIKE HIS HERO LAGUARDIA. HE WAS A BIT GRIM AND NOT ALL THAT SYMPATHETIC. BUT HE WAS GROWING ON NEW YORKERS BECAUSE HE WAS COMPETENT, HARDWORKING, AND AS FEISTY AS A CABDRIVER.[17]

—*Andrew Kirtzman, biographer*

If you think that I've run out of enthusiasm for the job because I'm a lame duck, watch out! This is my chance to do all of the things that I was too timid and restrained to do in the first administration.[18]

—*spoken during his 1997 reelection campaign*

I understand the game of politics that's played here, the game of racial politics. We're not perfect and we have a long way to go, but we're a lot better off than we were five, six years ago by being fair and evenhanded with people, and not rolling over for racial, religious, and ethnic exploitation.[19]

Giuliani is joined by then-wife Donna Hanover and children Andrew and Caroline on January 1, 1998, as he takes the oath of office from Judge Michael Mukasey for his second term as New York City mayor. (Mark Lennihan, AP/Wide World Photos)

A Bite out of Crime

RUDY GIULIANI MAY BE THE MOST SUCCESSFUL MAYOR IN AMERICA. HE LAUNCHED A ZERO-TOLERANCE ASSAULT ON LAWLESSNESS, TARGETING PUBLIC URINATORS AND TURNSTILE JUMPERS AS WELL AS KILLERS AND TRAFFICKERS, HELPING TO TRANSFORM NEW YORK CITY FROM A SCARY AND ANARCHIC WAR ZONE INTO ONE OF THE NATION'S SAFEST CITIES.[1]

—*Michael Grunwald*, New Republic *writer*

People throughout the world no longer see New York City as a national symbol of the plague of crime and violence. Now people see New York as a safe, decent place, and as a leader in fighting crime.

By enforcing the laws against aggressive panhandlers, squeegee operators, and graffiti vandals, we've made our city more livable, improving the quality of life.

Nearly twenty-five years of involvement in the fight against drugs has taught me many things; chief among them is that we must deal not only with the supply but also with the demand for drugs.

~

Over the last two years, we have seen unprecedented drops in serious crime in New York City. Combatting family violence has been an important part of our strategy.

~

When I was a U.S. Attorney, I prosecuted members of the Mafia. Some Italian-Americans criticized me for it, saying I was giving my community a bad name. I disagreed. From my perspective, I was helping the Italian-American community by demonstrating that the overwhelming majority of Italian-Americans reject the Mafia and everything it stands for.

~

The police rely on the information they obtain from a broad range of people, including illegal and undocumented immigrants who can catch those drug dealers and put them in prison.

⌒

Computer technologies allow the mapping of patterns and the establishment of causal relationships among different categories of crime.

⌒

People don't just want criminals arrested, they want no crime. They want a situation in which there is no reason to arrest people.

⌒

Just four years ago, we were known as one of the most dangerous cities in the country. Now, that's all changed. The FBI recently named us the safest city in the nation with a population (of) over one million people.

⌒

We've proven that reducing crime and improving the quality of life—besides being the right things to do—are also the keys to stimulating New York City's economy.

It wasn't that the organized crime leaders weren't being prosecuted—I know they were, because I was among those doing the prosecuting—but that people had come to accept the presence and influence of organized crime as intractable.

Organized crime figures are illegitimate people who would go on being illegitimate people if I got them off. I would not want to spend a lot of time with them, shake hands with them, have sidebar conferences with them. And become involved with people who are close to totally evil.[2]

THERE IS EMERGING A NEW NEW YORK THAT IS INCREASINGLY AUTHORITARIAN AND REPRESSIVE.[3]

—*Norman Siegel, New York*
Civil Liberty Union executive director

INCREASINGLY, YOU SEE MAYOR GIULIANI HANDLING DISSENT IN A MEAN-SPIRITED, BULLYING, AUTOCRATIC FASHION, AND INCREASINGLY USING THE POLICE AS A PRIVATE MAYORAL ARMY TO TARGET THOSE WHO DISAGREE WITH HIM.[4]

—*Ron Kuby, civil rights lawyer and activist*

Before you can enjoy any other civil rights, you have to be alive, you have to be able to walk around a city not afraid (of being) beaten, mugged, raped, or violated.

We cannot maintain, much less continue, our success in reducing crime unless we take steps now to change dramatically the balance in our criminal justice system so that the rights of victims and the rights of society are accorded at least as much, if not more, respect than the rights of the criminals.

Even one cop engaged in brutality or criminal conduct is one too many—and unfortunately it's more than one.

Long before he became New York City mayor, Giuliani made quite an impression as an aggressive attorney. He successfully took on organized crime and government corruption in getting an early start on cleaning up his beloved Big Apple. (AP/Wide World Photos)

Some people romanticize the way things were five or ten years ago. They have nostalgia for the old Times Square, for example. They think it was somehow charming to have graffiti on every wall and sex shops on every block. But remember what it was really like. Remember the fear and the disrespect for people's rights that went unchecked in that climate. It seemed like no one cared.

The very reason laws exist in the first place is so that people's rights can be protected, and that includes the right not to be disturbed, agitated, and abused by others.

~

Beginning with Roman law up through English common law to modern jurisprudence, much of the development of humanism has centered on a respect for property rights.

~

More cops do not necessarily reduce crime. In fact, you can have a lot more cops and have a lot more crime. It's what you do with the cops that reduces crime. It's the strategy that you utilize.

~

When somebody gets arrested for a crime, we should test their DNA in the same way we take their fingerprints. It's a method of identifying them. The innocent have nothing to fear from this. In fact, it is a very effective method of clearing people who are falsely accused of a crime or falsely accused of paternity.

~

Regardless of what is happening overseas, people have no right to harm anyone else or destroy property here in New York City. The best way to discourage people from doing this is to catch them and put them in prison, like we did the suspects in the attempted firebombing of the Bronx synagogue on the eve of Yom Kippur. We want to make certain that everyone understands that a line has to be drawn, and that the police department is prepared to arrest anyone who violates the law.

~

There are thousands of subtle ways that we interact with the law every day. Whether it is better law enforcement that has helped make the city a safer place or civil rights protections or the Bill of Rights, we learn valuable lessons and help shape the system through our participation.

~

I can vividly recall the 1970s and 1980s when left-wing Democratic administrations, with their "soft-on-crime" approach, allowed violent criminals and drug lords to rule our streets.[5]

~

The real core of the problem that we and other urban departments have is not brutality. I think brutality happens, but in the late 1990s it's an aberration.[6]

~

The most remarkable aspect of these continued crime declines is that the greatest impact is felt in the poorest and most depressed neighborhoods, proving that allocation of resources is based on need and not political considerations.[7]

~

New York, New York

Dream with me of a city better than the one we have been given. Believe with me that our problems can be reduced, not magically removed.

~

When things are bad, when times are tough, New Yorkers prove they are better and tougher.

~

For too long cities were defined by their problems. I believe—as I said before—that America's cities should be defined by their assets.

～

New York City is the capital of the world. And the presence of the United Nations makes that claim even more substantial.

～

New York City, like other American cities, was essentially written off as a symbol of urban decay. Yet we have proven the cynics wrong and shown what is possible. We did it by refusing to accept the notion that had pervaded city government for far too long—one of resignation and acceptance of the social and political problems that faced them.

～

People had written off urban America. No more! It's the cities that now are going through the resurgence.

～

Our challenge for the next four years, and into the next century, is to make sure that more and more New Yorkers have access to the same spirit of entrepreneurship and self-advancement that made the city great in the first place and that have led to our most recent turnaround.

⁓

New York City is now the city Americans most want to live in and visit. Could you have believed that four years ago?

⁓

Times Square is now a symbol and a reality of urban transcendence rather than decay.

⁓

One of the extraordinary and unique things about New York is that it is not a planned city. A commissar of planning did not devise New York. Nor was it built according to an original general scheme or overall organizing principle like Washington, D.C., or Paris. Yet it is better known and more successful than either of those cities, great and beautiful though they are. And its beauty and power emerge because it has always allowed scope for human creativity and genius.

⁓

The skyline of Manhattan, not planned, is a natural wonder of the world created by human beings. It keeps changing, but it continues to exude power, majesty, diversity, and beauty. It soars to the sky and reminds us all of the possibilities of human genius. It literally shows us the heights to which we can aspire. It reminds us that it is in the life of the spirit that we make our biggest contribution.

—spoken prior to September 11, 2001

We have transformed the city in so many ways because we refused to take the pessimism of the cynics to heart.

One of the most rewarding things for me as mayor has been to see a city that wasn't growing, and had unemployment of 30 to 40 percent in the construction industry, turn into a city that is growing up all over again.

I keep a national magazine cover describing New York City in 1990 as "the Rotting Apple," a city in decline. And at that time, people in the city of New York accepted it. They accepted the idea that this was our lot in life: that we were an old city that had seen our greatest days.

~

Now we understand much more clearly why people from all over the globe want to come to New York, and to America . . . why they always have, and why they always will. It's called freedom, equal protection under law, respect for human life, and the promise of opportunity.

~

We're a city where people look different, talk different, think different. But we're a city at one with all of the people at the World Trade Center, and with all of America. We love our diversity, and we love our freedom.

~

Nothing can match summertime in New York, which is why the city is such a magnet for tourists.

As the weather gets warmer, many of our thoughts turn to baseball, barbecues, walks in the park, and other enjoyable outdoor activities. I would like to ask you to consider another outdoor activity during this spring and summer—taking steps to protect yourself and your neighbors from the possible return of West Nile virus.

I believe that President Clinton's being in New York—and particularly being in Harlem—is a very good thing. I think his presence here will say something very significant about where Harlem is now, not only to the people of New York, but to the rest of the country.

No place in America has this kind of excitement. You can't match this.[1]

New York City is committed to the care and preservation of its trees. They play a vital role in keeping our neighborhoods beautiful, in helping to keep our air clean, and providing shade for community residents. They enhance our quality of life by offering a little peace and tranquility in a bustling, hectic city.

New Yorkers have always braved the hardships of life with a true flair. They did so because New York was an exciting and stunning place to live, to work, and to visit.[2]

Schools and Education

We must do away with the practice of so-called "social promotion," whereby students who don't meet academic standards for promotion from one grade to the next are moved ahead anyway. This system cheats our children.

∼

We must make restoring safety in the schools a top priority, because children cannot learn when they are afraid—nor can teachers teach in a classroom ruled by fear.

∼

Thomas Jefferson once noted that "No democracy can function effectively without an educated and informed populace." And ultimately that really is the point.

⌒

Education is 25 percent of the city's budget . . . but it's 100 percent of our city's future.

⌒

A culture of unaccountability is being replaced with a culture of performance.

⌒

Teaching a child to read is giving that child the key to a future of hope and fulfillment.

⌒

The arts should be equally important as math, history, and science. The arts inspire hope.

⌒

In order to become fully functioning participants in
American society, sufficient knowledge of technology and
computers has become a prerequisite.

~

We must end the policy of allowing people seven years
to graduate from a regular high school, which means we
have twenty-one-year-olds in the same school building
as fourteen-year-old students. That's demoralizing to the
students themselves, the students around them, and
their teachers.

~

The new educational philosophy in this city must be that we
will do what works for the children—rather than perpetuating
the old way of doing things simply because it is familiar.

~

Bilingual education should be restored to its original well-
intended purpose. It should be allowed for a short period of
transition (a year or two at most), with most of this time
spent in intense English immersion programs instead of
career-long bilingual programs with no definable goal.

~

By eliminating any meaningful standards of admission and continually defining down standards for continuation, the entire meaning and value of a college education has been put in jeopardy for the many who are ready, willing, and able to meet and exceed higher standards.

We too should teach civility as a subject within the classroom—ideally, as part of civics classes. Unfortunately, there is no such thing as a civics class anymore. That's a shame.

Academia can create opportunities, innovation, creativity, and growth that business can't possibly accomplish.

People go to Milwaukee to see how to fix schools. They go to Chicago for that. They go to Cleveland. And they go to Florida. Because in those places, people are doing innovative and creative things that take real courage. New York City is not, and our inaction is doing a horrible disservice to our children.

We don't need a board of education. We don't need boards of education. We need schools. We need teachers. We need principals. We need standards of accountability. We need to get parents more involved. We need more books. We need more computers. These are the things we need. We don't need boards. They distract, and they do even worse than that.

Last year I advocated blowing it up (the board of education office building). Alright, well, I'm softening up. I'm becoming an easier guy. We're not going to blow it up—we're going to sell it.

~

You only get one chance to educate a child, and if you screw it up, then it's very hard to correct it later.

~

There's no question that many parents feel, quite correctly, that their children are not getting the education that they deserve and that they should have. And that feeling is the strongest among parents who are the poorest, and without resources to, in essence, buy a much better and higher quality education for their children.

~

Every good school is an overcrowded school. If a school is an excellent school, then everybody wants to go there.

～

After a very long battle, we've ended principal tenure and replaced it with a system of performance-based contracts that reward the principals who are doing a good job and enable us to remove the principals who are failing our children.

～

There are hundreds of studies that indicate that American students are falling behind their European and Asian counterparts, and that's something that should concern all of us. Part of the problem is due to the fact that there's been a decline in public education in American cities.

～

One of the things I enjoy most about being mayor is visiting schoolchildren, reading with them, and hearing about what they want to be when they grow up.[1]

⌒

Schoolchildren are harassed by school officials for praying on their own time because schools are terrified of lawsuits by the ACLU.[2]

⌒

We should teach tolerance and respect, but we should do it with materials that are sensible. We don't have to get into artificial insemination at seven years old.[3]

⌒

I personally believe that it's important to have your religious part of your education every single day.[4]

⌒

New York's Finest
and Bravest

New York City has lots of heroes and lots of legends. Our most important heroes are our police officers and our firefighters.

~

The police power is the power to provide for the health, the safety, and the well-being of people in the community.

~

Respect takes root and grows when it is mutual. Those who want more respect from the police must be willing to give that same respect in return.

~

Giuliani and city police commissioner Howard Safir (right) meet with reporters from a makeshift command center at Shea Stadium after a transformer fire had knocked out power to a hundred thousand Queens residents for six hours in May 1996. (Todd Plitt, AP/Wide World Photos)

Supporting the police is a way to save lives. But you have to be willing to withstand criticism and ignore public opinion polls that say you're unpopular when you're doing it. If we're going to continue to reduce crime and save lives, then the political leaders of the city have to understand this principle.

Firefighting is still an enormously dangerous job—it always will be—and that's why we owe them the best equipment possible . . . because they do something that most of us in this room could never do. They put their lives at risk to save you, to save your children, to save your relatives, to save the people that you love. We see a fire and we run away. They see a fire and they run in and pull your child out. And they don't ask the questions that politicians fight about all the time.

Without courage, nothing else can really happen. And there is no better example, none, than the courage of the fire department of the city of New York.

I want you to know that the prayers of every single New York Yorker, I believe every single American, are with you. Your willingness to go forward undaunted in the most difficult of circumstances is an inspiration to all of us. It sends a signal that our hearts are broken, no question about that, but our hearts continue to beat, and they beat very, very strongly.[1]

—*speaking at a city fire department promotion ceremony less than a week after the terrorist attacks on the World Trade Center*

Never forget that police officers put their lives on the line every day to keep you and your loved ones safe from harm. At the very least, they deserve your thanks and your support.

Every firefighter's family understands the risks that their loved ones take when they put on the uniform of the New York City Fire Department. They hope and they pray that no harm will come to them. But that never lessens the shock or the sorrow that overwhelms a family when one of our city's Bravest dies in the line of duty.

In the last great attack on America, the attack on Pearl Harbor, the first casualties were the members of our United States Navy. They wore a uniform like you do. In this war, the first large casualties are being experienced by the New York City Fire Department. The Navy regrouped, it fought back, it won the Battle of Midway, and it turned the tide of the battle in the Pacific, after it had been devastated. The New York City Fire Department is being re-formed today. It reminds me of battlefield commissions during a time of war.

Without courage, nothing else can really happen.[2]

We can't knock this police department all the way off course. This is not the police department that some of the extremists are painting. This is not the KKK.[3]

There's never been a mayor who understands the psyche of the police department the way I do.[4]

Coming to America

New York City is a beacon of hope to millions around the world and here in America. New York City has provided generations of immigrants the opportunity to rise up . . . to become a part of the American dream.

~

The most diverse place in the city is the borough of Queens, where New Yorkers from South America, the West Indies, Africa, Asia, and Europe are building our city's and our nation's future.

~

All of them came here because they want to create a better life for themselves . . . they want to achieve . . . and they challenge each of us to do better.

Potential university presidents are still arriving in America.

History shows that America goes through periods where people become fearful of immigration. But eventually we return to the recognition that new Americans are good for our country.

We are constantly being reinvented, not just by the free flow of ideas, but by the free flow of people.

If I could take you out to Kennedy Airport—which in many ways is the Ellis Island of today—you would see people coming to America from many different parts of the world. In some ways they may look different and speak differently than the immigrants who came through Ellis Island . . . but the look in their eyes is the same.

Basically, new immigrants to America are no different than the old immigrants to America.

⁓

The fact is, immigration makes economic sense. Immigrants work hard; in New York City, foreign-born males are 10 percent more likely to be employed than native-born males.

⁓

Competition is the heart of the Republican philosophy . . . and immigration clearly helps New York City compete.

⁓

Illegal immigration is a different matter. I do not defend it. No one should break the law.

⁓

Giuliani, himself a grandson of immigrants, long took an A-OK approach when it came to accommodating immigrants coming to New York City for a new life. (Adam Nadel, AP/Wide World Photos)

Preventing illegal immigration is the job of the federal government.

~

It takes courage and ambition to leave your native country and start a new life in a new land.

~

My grandfather, Rodolfo Giuliani, arrived in New York City without much money in his pocket, but with a dream in his heart. And his dream of freedom and success became my dream.

~

The spirit of our city is renewed over and over again by new people who come here wanting to make a better life for themselves and their families, and then they make life better for all of us.

~

Most Americans are citizens by birth. Immigrants are Americans by choice. They approach our country with a very personal understanding of the value of equal opportunity and freedom.

~

Rudy His Own Self

Whenever we discuss, debate, or disagree, you can always persuade me to change my mind, if you can persuade me your approach is better for the people we serve.

I love New York. I'm very proud to be a New Yorker, and I am honored that the people of this great city have chosen me to be their mayor. I was born in Brooklyn. I've lived in Queens and Manhattan. I went to school in Brooklyn, the Bronx, and Manhattan. The only place where I haven't lived or gone to school is Staten Island. To compensate, I've spent more time in Staten Island than any mayor in the history of the city.

Thank you, New Yorkers, for reelecting me to a job I love so much.

—upon being reelected New York City mayor in 1997

THIS FELLA IS GETTING THINGS DONE. HE'S NOT AFRAID TO STEP ON SOME TOES. SOMETIMES YOU AGREE WITH HIM, SOMETIMES YOU DISAGREE WITH HIM, BUT AT LEAST YOU KNOW HIS POSITION.[1]

—Gary Muhrcke, who owns a shoe store opposite Bryant Park, which was once a drug haven behind the New York Public Library and is now a place where office workers relax

To me civility and niceness are not the same thing. Civility is the basic respect you have to have for the law. I actually think I am a very polite person.[2]

MY HUSBAND IS THE MOST VIRILE MAN.[3]

—Donna Hanover, before she became Rudy's ex-wife

~

The fact is there is a lot more scrutiny of people's private lives than was the case ten, fifteen, twenty years ago. If it connects, in honesty and good faith, to the performance of their job; if you can find some connection between a problem they have in their private life or an issue they have in their private life, and the way they are doing their job; then it's a legitimate [issue]. If it doesn't, then it really is just to satisfy someone's prurient interest, and that's kind of a sad way for our society to go, and a sad way for journalism or politics to go.[4]

—expressing his disdain for media coverage of his marital problems

~

RUDY HAS DONE THE CITY A GREAT SERVICE OVER THE LAST
EIGHT YEARS. I DON'T THINK THERE'S ANY QUESTION BUT THAT
BY MOST MEASURES THIS CITY IS MUCH MORE LIVABLE FOR ALMOST
ALL ITS CITIZENS THAN IT WAS EIGHT YEARS AGO. RUDY WAS THE
BENEFICIARY OF A GOOD ECONOMY. RUDY WAS THE BENEFICIARY
OF WASHINGTON FOCUSING ON HELPING CITIES. RUDY WAS THE
BENEFICIARY OF SOME DEMOGRAPHIC TRENDS. BUT TO NOT GIVE
RUDY CREDIT FOR MAKING A DIFFERENCE IN THIS CITY SEEMS TO
ME RIDICULOUS.[5]

—*Michael R. Bloomberg, who was later
elected New York City mayor as Giuliani's successor*

I take a different view of someone comparing me to Adolf
Hitler than when someone calls me a jerk.[6]

I don't regard associations of my people that support me as
fascists as a light matter . . . But it's ultimately the results
that matter.[7]

I don't get offended any longer when people call me crazy.
But I wonder about a doctor running a methadone program
who, when a mayor raises the idea that we should end
methadone, which is a way of keeping people dependent,
describes my idea as crazy.[8]

This is wonderful. I think the more ticker-tape parades
I can have during the time that I'm mayor, the more great
memories I'm going to have later on.[9]

—spoken just before former astronaut and
U.S. senator John Glenn got another ticker-tape
parade in New York following his return to space in 1998

If the city were to grant permits to everyone who wants to
have a parade, all the city would do is have parades.[10]

—explaining why he rejected applications
for a number of parade permits, including an
activist group wanting to honor World AIDS Day

I spent a lot of years being a lawyer, assistant U.S. Attorney, U.S. Attorney. I've dealt with a lot of disturbed people; sometimes you can just hear it in their voice.[11]

—on his call-in show, speaking to a listener

It's better to do the right thing, prove the city is manageable, so no one can ever say it isn't again.[12]

—on his being admired more than loved

Yes, I played hookey to play baseball, and somehow I survived it and became mayor.[13]

I have a pretty good sense of the media, of the direction and how it spins things, and I also have a sense of the things I could say that would quickly make me more popular, but I don't believe them, so I'm not going to say them.[14]

I think I'm taking New York City into the next century
in much better shape than I found it. If people like me
personally, thank you. If you don't, I don't really care.[15]

⌒

I know that they've called me a bully. I know that they
called me all kinds of names. You want my reaction to it? I
won't quit.[16]

⌒

I was a crammer in college. I read very fast. This was during
the era of President Kennedy's speed-reading course, the
Evelyn Wood speed-reading course. I got all this material
about the course, and it did increase my reading speed.[17]

⌒

My father used to have this expression, which was that he
didn't want me to love him, he wanted me to respect him.
After I respected him, I would learn to love him. I never quite
understood how that worked out at home, but it seemed to
me a very good philosophy for running an organization.[18]

⌒

Rudy and son Andrew partake in the celebration after the New York Yankees beat the Atlanta Braves in six games to win the 1996 World Series. (John Bazemore, AP/Wide World Photos)

My dad taught me a lot of really good things, and he was a wonderful man, but no—as I've told, you know, my son, daughter—no father is perfect. You know fathers—fathers make mistakes and fathers are human beings, and I tend to think now that love is more important than I thought it was.[19]

I used to hide my personal side. People thought I was a machine. People want to get to know you, to get to feel you. I was holding part of myself back.[20]

Not Welfare;
Workfare

Our workfare program recognizes that welfare is supposed to be a temporary helping hand, not a way of life.

⌒

We must replace the sense of entitlement which is pervasive throughout our society—from the elderly to the affluent to the poor—with the principle of reciprocity.

⌒

When I look to the future, I see a city where a culture of dependency and a culture of hopelessness is replaced by a culture of self-sufficiency and a culture of self-respect.

⌒

At the core of our approach to welfare reform is the basic concept of a social contract—that for every right there is a duty, for every benefit an obligation.

What is progressive about people becoming
dependent? There is nothing progressive about
welfare.

⁓

When I suggested people in emergency shelters be
assigned to work, there were some that criticized
that this was attempting to "punish" people. Their
attitude is very revealing as a significant difference
in philosophy: whereas they consider work
punishment, our administration considers work
an opportunity for improvement and for growth.

⁓

A job well done restores a sense of dignity,
independence, and self-esteem that no social
program can match.

⁓

Remaining in the workforce is better than letting people drop out of the discipline of work for months, years, and sometimes a lifetime. The consequences for them, and their children, are disastrous.

~

We want to keep in people's lives the discipline of getting up in the morning, getting dressed, and going to a job. Not because we love people less, but because we have progressed to loving them more deeply, more maturely.

~

I'm a Catholic, but somehow I got the Protestant work ethic.

~

Work is what allows you to take care of yourself and your family, and to achieve your dreams.

Sports and Culture

The New York Yankees are the greatest franchise in sports, and New York is the greatest city in the world—and the Capital of the World.

~

The Yankees have created much of the history and legend of baseball, and now this 1996 Yankees team has written a new and glorious chapter in that history and legend.

~

And their victory is an inspiration for all of us. It is a metaphor for a city whose people perform best under pressure. It is a metaphor for a city that is undergoing a great renaissance.

~

I'm sure all of us here can remember the first time we went to a baseball field to see our first professional game. For a young boy from Brooklyn, I remember it like it was yesterday. My father took me all the way from Brooklyn to Yankee Stadium,to watch the Yankees play the Red Sox. Joe DiMaggio was playing center field for the Yankees, and his brother Dominick was playing center field for the Red Sox. They hit singles to each other. I found it very odd that brothers would be on different teams.

~

Joe DiMaggio ultimately transcended even the Yankees and New York City. He became the symbol ultimately not of a specific team or city or place but of what we perceive to be a simpler America.

~

Having the Olympic Games in the City of New York would be the perfect culmination of the ongoing renaissance of our city. We have transformed our city from a symbol of all that was wrong with urban America to a symbol of hope, success, and innovation that is looked to—and learned from—by cities around the world.

—addressing New York City's bid for the 2012 Summer Olympics

Not only do sports teach things that are useful throughout life—such as teamwork, discipline, and a respect for rules—physical activity also is essential to a long and healthy life. Involvement in school athletics is related to higher grade point averages as well.

Subway Series fever has gripped New York. The city is captivated by the Bronx-Queens showdown. This is a dream come true for New York baseball fans.

*—referring to the 2000 World Series
showdown between the Mets and Yankees*

Thank God, it's still as exciting as the first time I ever saw a game. And thank God the hot dogs are as delicious.[1]

Ⅽ⌣

The greatest and most successful cities have always been those in which the arts have flourished and grown.

Ⅽ⌣

It is in the music, drama, dance, paintings, sculpture, and architecture created, and in the writings of our philosophers, theologians, poets, novelists, and historians, that we define ourselves for future generations.

Ⅽ⌣

We're the Cultural Capital of the World. We're the place where the performing arts, the visual arts—all of the arts—have been developed to a stage that's defining our civilization.

Ⅽ⌣

An aggressively hateful antireligion exhibit (that) desecrates the Virgin Mary![2]

—*describing the Brooklyn Museum's "Sensation" exhibit*

~

It offends me. The idea of, in the name of art, having a city-subsidized building have so-called works of art in which people are throwing elephant dung at a picture of the Virgin Mary is sick. If somebody wants to do that privately, well, that's what the First Amendment is all about. The city shouldn't have to pay for sick stuff.[3]

~

I guess it's okay to use taxpayer funds to subsidize religious expression so long as it involves the desecration of religious symbols.[4]

~

Business

If the economy needs a jobs program, reduce taxes to create jobs for poor people.[1]

~

Over the past four years, we've worked hard to create a climate in which New York City's businesses can thrive. We've realized that government's role is to ensure that there are open and competitive markets and to give businesses the freedom and the confidence to grow on their own.

~

We've been able to move forward together because, block by block and neighborhood by neighborhood, people are no longer afraid to open businesses. Businesspeople are no longer afraid that every investment they make in their communities will be fundamentally jeopardized by crime.

~

City government is getting out of the way of business and reinvesting in the hardworking New Yorkers who make this the most successful city in the nation.

~

The mob tax inflated prices for everyone, lowered the quality of goods and services, and forced too many honest people to live in fear. The perception and reality of this problem provided yet another reason for businesses and investors—and jobs—to stay away from New York City.

~

Investors once again have confidence in the
fundamental fiscal strength of our city and
confidence in our future.

～

Businesses invest in communities. They build
structures that anchor neighborhoods. They serve
as ambassadors of our city to other cities around
the country and other nations around the world.

～

The less government control there is, the more
you're willing to give back to private enterprise
and to people, the more you can have real growth
and a sense of freedom and opportunity.

～

Wall Street has been instrumental in helping to create budget surpluses for the city, but our job gains have been broad-based in a wide range of different neighborhoods and industries.

～

All New Yorkers need to have the confidence that our economy is run by the men and women who do the hard work—that, based on the rules of a free market, the quality of goods and services are pushed up, and the prices are pushed down.

～

His Prostate Cancer

Good morning. I was diagnosed yesterday with a—with prostate cancer. It's a treatable form of prostate cancer. It was diagnosed at an early stage. It came about as a result of taking a PSA test about two and a half weeks ago. The PSA was elevated. So I took antibiotics for a while. Took the PSA test again. It remained elevated, so I went in for a biopsy yesterday, and the biopsy revealed that several of the samples, thank goodness not all and not most, had indications of cancer.

~

The doctor called me on the telephone yesterday afternoon and then I met with him afterwards. We talked about it in person. He told me on the telephone, you know, (about) the test. I keep getting positive and negative mixed up. I kind of think of negative as bad and positive as good, so when he told me it was positive, it took me a second to figure out: Oh, gee, that is not so good.

⌒

This is not the right time for me to run for office. What I should do is to put my health first.[1]

—on dropping out of the 2000 Senate race

⌒

Each year, close to two hundred thousand American men are diagnosed with prostate cancer. Prostate cancer is the second-leading cause—after lung cancer—of cancer deaths in men. From my own experience, I can assure you that early intervention is the key to fighting this deadly disease.

⌒

BEFORE HE SEEMED LIKE A DICTATOR . . . LIKE IRON. BUT NOW HE
LOOKS LIKE HE WANTS TO CRY. CAN YOU SEE THAT? RUDY CRYING?[2]
                                    —*unnamed New York auto mechanic*

Someone said to me today, "God works in strange ways,
and if you had run for the Senate and gotten elected, you
wouldn't be here right now." So, I don't know. But it must
have changed me in some way.[3]

I'm a fortunate man. God has given me a lot. Whatever
obstacles that are placed in your way, I think the way to
deal with it is to try to figure out how to make it make you
a better person.[4]

I think I understand myself a lot better.[5]

You can't put a time frame on this, you have to make the decision when you're ready to make it.

It makes you figure out what you're all about and what's really important to you and what should be important to you—you know, where the core of you really exists. And I guess because I've been in public life so long and politics, I used to think the core of me was in politics, probably. It isn't.[6]

I would urge everyone to get the PSA test. There is nothing painful about the PSA test. It's a blood test. . . . If the PSA is normal or low, you don't have a problem. If it is high, then you should have it tested and find out.

Just the contemplation of it for the last two weeks makes you think about what's important in life, and what are the most important things. But, you know, you should be thinking about that anyway.[7]

September 11 and the Aftermath

Within moments after the first plane struck, ordinary men and women showed extraordinary bravery in assisting one another to safety, even at the cost of their own lives. Our fire fighters and police officers have personified courage, and though the losses to their ranks have been terrible, they have set the example for the rest of us by continuing to work with renewed vigor.

~

People walked, ran, did all the things they had to do to get away. But there wasn't the kind of thing that fiction and movies predicted if there was ever going to be a nuclear or chemical attack, which is people would trample each other in panic. There was fear, but no panic.[1]

~

President George W. Bush is flanked by Giuliani on his right and city fire commissioner Thomas Van Essen on his left during a tour of the World Trade Center rubble, three days after the September 11, 2001, terrorist attacks. (Doug Mills, AP/Wide World Photos)

FROM THE ASHES OF THE WORLD TRADE CENTER, THE MAYOR OF THE CITY OF NEW YORK HAS EMERGED AS THE EMBODIMENT OF GRACE UNDER PRESSURE. HIS EMERGENCE WAS LITERAL. AS DEBRIS CASCADED FROM THE TWIN TOWERS, GIULIANI AND SEVERAL OF HIS TOP ADVISERS WERE STUCK IN A DOWNTOWN COMMAND CENTER WHERE THEY HAD BEEN LEADING THE CITY'S INITIAL EMERGENCY RESPONSE EFFORTS.[2]

—Deroy Murdock, news reporter

New Yorkers are very unified in their reaction, which is horror, shock, determination. And I think they're probably more patriotic than they've been in a long time.[3]

~

When you see it from the air, you realize how devastating it is, how massive. I think seeing that smoke come out, it just makes you angry, and it makes you determined.[4]

~

There should be a memorial, and there should also be office space. It's the most important financial district in the world, and you want to build on that.[5]

~

THE MAYOR IS ABLE TO DO THIS BECAUSE HE IS ALWAYS
LOOKING FORWARD. THE ABILITY TO DO THAT HAS
ALWAYS GOTTEN US THROUGH HARD TIMES. IT MAY BE
ONE OF THE FEW ASPECTS OF THIS ADMINISTRATION
THAT IS OVERLOOKED.[6]

—*Joseph J. Lhota, deputy mayor, referring to*
Giuliani's immediate hands-on involvement

THERE IS NO DOUBT THAT GIULIANI IS THE MAN
YOU WANT IN CHARGE OF THIS SITUATION. EVERYONE
KNOWS WE WANT A RAISE, BUT IN THIS SITUATION IT
IS LIKE HE IS THE ONLY ONE WHO SEEMS TO TAKE
COMMAND.[7]

—*Sgt. Michael Hanrahan, New York City policeman*

HE MOVES ABOUT THE STRICKEN CITY LIKE A GOD.
PEOPLE WANT TO BE IN HIS PRESENCE. THEY WANT TO
TOUCH HIM. THEY WANT TO PRAISE HIM.[8]

—*Bob Herbert*, New York Times *writer*

One of the reasons we've been able to handle this at all, is we've had all these drills for four, five, six years. . . . For about a year now, my deputy mayor, Joe Lhota, and I keep complaining that we spent so much money on Y2K, and maybe it was a big fraud. He said to me, "All of that planning is actually helping us now."[9]

We will strive now to save as many people as possible and to send a message that the city of New York—and the United States of America—is much stronger than any group of barbaric terrorists. I want the people of New York to be an example.[10]

NO ONE EMBODIED THAT SPIRIT MORE THAN THE MAYOR, RUDOLPH W. GIULIANI, A COMPLEX MAN, CAPABLE OF DISPLAYING EXTRAORDINARY LEADERSHIP ONE MINUTE AND BREATHTAKING PETTINESS THE NEXT. IN THIS CRISIS, MR. GIULIANI WAS MAJESTIC. HE RALLIED NEW YORKERS AND CALMED THEM, INSPIRED THEM AND CONSOLED THEM. MANY NEW YORKERS REACTED TO THE POSTPONEMENT OF THE MAYORAL PRIMARY WITH WISTFUL WISHES THAT THEY COULD DO AWAY WITH THE TERM LIMITS FORCING MR. GIULIANI FROM OFFICE.[11]

—*Clyde Haberman*, New York Times *writer*

IF YOU'RE LIKE ME AND YOU'RE
WATCHING AND YOU'RE CONFUSED AND
DEPRESSED AND IRRITATED AND ANGRY
AND FULL OF GRIEF AND YOU DON'T
KNOW HOW TO BEHAVE AND YOU'RE NOT
SURE WHAT TO DO, BECAUSE WE'VE NEVER
BEEN THROUGH THIS BEFORE, ALL YOU
HAD TO DO AT ANY MOMENT WAS WATCH
THE MAYOR. WATCH HOW THIS GUY
BEHAVED. WATCH HOW THIS GUY
CONDUCTED HIMSELF. . . . RUDOLPH
GIULIANI IS THE PERSONIFICATION
OF COURAGE.[12]

—*David Letterman, host of* The Late Show,
*during his emotional opening for his first
show back after the September 11 attacks*

Life is going to go on. Both the life of the city and the life of the department. We have very important work to do today, tomorrow, in the months and in the years ahead.

~

The spirit of democracy is stronger than these cowardly terrorists.

~

The proud Twin Towers that once crowned our famous skyline no longer stand. But our skyline will rise again. In the words of President George W. Bush, "We will rebuild New York City."

~

To those who say that our city will never be the same, I say you are right. It will be better.

~

All of the victims of this tragedy were innocent. All of them were heroes.

~

The Bible says [John 15:13], "Greater love hath no man than this, that a man lay down his life for his friends." Our brave New York City firefighters . . . New York City police officers . . . Port Authority police officers . . . EMS workers . . . health-care workers . . . court officers . . . and uniformed service members . . . they laid down their lives for strangers. They were inspired by their sense of duty and their love for humanity. As they raced into the Twin Towers and the other buildings to save lives, they didn't stop to ask how rich or poor the person was, they didn't stop to ask what religion, what race, what nationality. They just raced in to save their fellow human beings. They are the best example of love that we have in our society.

~

We humbly bow our heads and we ask God to bless the city of New York, and we ask God to bless the United States of America.

~

This was not just an attack on the city of New York or on the United States of America. It was an attack on the very idea of a free, inclusive, and civil society. It was a direct assault on the founding principles of the United Nations itself.

⁓

Terrorism is based on the persistent and deliberate violation of fundamental human rights. With bullets and bombs— and now with hijacked airplanes—terrorists deny the dignity of human life.

⁓

Look at that destruction, that massive, senseless, cruel loss of human life . . . and then I ask you to look in your hearts and recognize that there is no room for neutrality on the issue of terrorism. You're either with civilization or with terrorists.

⁓

On one side is democracy, the rule of law, and respect for human life; on the other is tyranny, arbitrary executions, and mass murder. We're right and they're wrong. It's as simple as that.

⁓

Those who practice terrorism—murdering or victimizing innocent civilians—lose any right to have their cause understood by decent people and lawful nations.

~

I say to people across the country and around the world: If you were planning to come to New York sometime in the future, come here now. Come to enjoy our thousands of restaurants, museums, theaters, sporting events, and shopping . . . but also come to take a stand against terrorism.

~

With each passing day since the vicious and unprovoked attacks of September 11, Americans have developed a clearer understanding of the fact that we now face an enemy unlike any other that we have faced in the past. We confront an elusive enemy whose methods are based upon undermining our freedoms through fear.

~

The resilience of life in New York City is the ultimate sign of defiance to terrorism.

Thousands of tests have been taken for anthrax throughout the city; the number of confirmed exposures has been extremely low; and all of those who have been found to have anthrax have fully recovered. This is an eminently treatable disease whose primary impact has been the spread of fear.

We must remember that panic can be more dangerous than the disease itself. We are encountering many of these threats for the first time, but America and other nations across the world have triumphed over far greater challenges in the past.

Fall is one of the best times of the year to be in New York City, because it is a time of anticipation, excitement, and celebration. After all that we've endured and all that we've accomplished over the last month and a half, the Yankees' success this October is a greater source of civic pride than ever before. Joe Torre said it best when he described the "NY" logo on their hats and uniforms as representing more than just the team. That logo is for every New Yorker, every American, and every person around the world who loves freedom and refuses to be intimidated by the barbaric acts of terrorists.

They were able to accept much more as part of their way of life, than we are being asked to accept, in the 1940s when they were bombed every day and still went about their living and showed a great example of bravery and courage to the rest of the world.[13]

—referring to how Londoners went
about their lives during World War II

⁓

The scope of it surprised him, particularly from the helicopter. He just looked at it, absorbed it, and said, "Oh, my."[14]

—talking about President Bush's reaction
during his first helicopter tour of Ground Zero

⁓

It is a true testament to our resolve that only seven weeks after the worst attack on American soil, New York turned out in the millions to support marathon runners from throughout the world. Our enthusiasm was rewarded by seeing the Yankees play in some of the most thrilling World Series games in the history of our national pastime. And our strong determination not to let terrorists undermine our principles of freedom has already reaped many benefits.

⁓

Over the last couple of months we have had much to cry about and much to cheer about, but the one constant throughout this entire time has been our immense feeling of pride— pride for what we've endured and accomplished.

Rudy Redux (A-Z)

ACCOUNTABILITY

In order to instill a sense of accountability in government, we closely measure the performance of our public health agencies.

~

I love charts. I love charts because they take the sometimes amorphous job that a government does, and they focus things so that you can evaluate people and agencies, and so that you can establish real accountability.

~

AMERICAN FLIGHT 587

The best thing people should do is suspend judgment.
People should do their normal activities. The city is open
for business.[1]

> —addressing possible public concern about
> the cause of the November 2001 crash of
> Flight 587 minutes after taking off from Kennedy Airport

We have to learn how to grieve and how to enjoy ourselves
in the same day. Maybe that's a lesson for life.[2]

Two parts of the city were hit particularly hard by the
crash—the Dominican-American neighborhood of
Washington Heights and the Rockaway section of
Queens. These two communities are bolstered by their
strong religious faith, their patriotism and honor for
country, and their understanding of the importance
of a strong community.

Eight years as New York City mayor put Giuliani up close and personal to numerous disasters, including three major airplane crashes. Here he speaks to newsmen at JFK Airport on September 2, 1998, after Swissair Flight 111 bound for Geneva, Switzerland, crashed in the Atlantic Ocean off Nova Scotia. (Ron Frehm, AP/Wide World Photos)

THE AMERICAN WAY

The test of being an American is not a test of one's ethnic background, religion, or race, it's a much more fundamental test—a test of whether you truly believe that "all men are created equal."

~

CABBIES

MAYOR GIULIANI VOWS TO HAVE COPS WITH HAMMERS AND CHISELS PRY THE MEDALLIONS RIGHT OFF THE HOOD OF ANY CAB IN THE DEMONSTRATION.[3]

—News Radio 88 report

~

If they would like to stay home forever, they can stay home forever as far as I'm concerned. The city will function very well without them.[4]

—addressing cabbies after their one-day strike in protest of his assessment of their collective behavior as reckless

~

CHANGE

You have to always be willing to challenge yourself to change. If you don't, then you can't govern a city like New York.[5]

~

CITY TRAFFIC

Every breakdown of the rules of the road contributes to a climate of disorder, a climate in which drivers, pedestrians, and bicyclists begin to fear each other rather than one in which we all respect one another and try hard to make our streets work for everyone.

~

CIVIL RIGHTS

The most fundamental of civil rights is the guarantee that government can give you a reasonable degree of safety. I was very heavily criticized by the people who used to run New York City government because they said I really didn't understand civil rights. I thought their criticism aptly describes the philosophical difference of my approach and those of my predecessors.

~

CIVILITY

Civility is about the responsibility you have as a public official and a citizen. You have to work. You have to obey laws. You have to consider the rights of others.[6]

〜

COMMUNITY

It's important to have a civil society in the smallest of towns, where mutual respect often becomes the anchor of community. It's even more important in as large, dense, diverse, vibrant, and complex a city as New York City.

〜

We must recognize that our relationship to one another as brother and sister goes deeper than our racial, ethnic, or religious identity . . . It is our common humanity . . . our identity as human beings.

〜

Across the nation people are reevaluating their expectations for local, state, and federal policies. There is an increasing recognition that government must play a secondary role to families and individuals in resolving social problems.

〜

It's time we recognized that prejudice and stereotyping can emanate from any direction . . . from any community . . . from any neighborhood.

Society's biggest problems will ultimately be solved by society's smallest units. It is from the communities, the neighborhoods, the block associations, the churches, the schools, the families, and from within each individual that the changes that will build a better society will come. This is something that the Citizens Committee of New York City has understood since its founding in 1975.

When we further the quality of life and advance the city of New York as a more civilized city, we reinforce the notion that all of our actions affect each other.[7]

Government at a distance is bound to be ineffective. It cannot accurately reflect the aspirations, needs, and desires of local communities. The result is often that people feel alienated, angry, and less connected to the political process.

COURAGE

A gifted mind is nothing without a strong, loving, courageous soul.[8]

~

DAD

I miss my father every day of my life. And he's a very, very important reason for why I'm standing here as the mayor of New York City.[9]

~

DISEASE CONTROL

The more dead mosquitoes, the better.

~

DONNA HANOVER

This is very, very painful. For quite some time it's probably been apparent that Donna and I lead, in many ways, independent and separate lives. It's been a very painful road.[10]

~

DRUG ABUSE

Most of the people who are treated for drugs are forced to be treated because they get arrested. We need to have large numbers of people seeking treatment for drugs, and we need to do things to encourage them to do so if we are going to turn around the problem.

∼

To break an addiction requires enormous effort, tremendous commitment, and if you're willing to make it, we'll supply the program for you.[11]

∼

Drug abuse enslaves the mind and destroys the soul, causing people to abandon their duties, their children, their friends, their jobs, their education—everything that is worthwhile in life, everything that makes a city great.

∼

We get to a drug-free America by arresting the people who are selling drugs, putting them in jail for a very, very long time, and recognizing the fact that people who sell those dangerous drugs are very much like murderers because they take people's lives from them, and treating that very seriously.

THE ECONOMY

The whole purpose and approach of my administration has been to restructure our economy in New York City to revitalize the private sector and make the role of government supportive rather than intrusive. To make us a pro-business city—because encouraging business growth means encouraging job growth.

FAITH

I think America needs more faith and more respect for religious traditions . . . not less.[12]

FREEDOM

Freedom is about authority. Freedom is about the willingness of every single human being to cede to lawful authority a great deal of discretion about what you do and how you do it.[13]

GOVERNMENT

The best way to restore the public's shaken faith in government and in national institutions is to speak realistically about the challenges we face and what government can do to help individuals achieve their goals. Samuelson calls this new era "the age of responsibility."

Accountability translates to a government that is willing to be measured.

One of the legacies of the Roosevelt administration and the depression was the tendency of people to look first and foremost to the government to solve their problems. And President Reagan changed the mind of America about this.

Our city had to be sued to open emergency shelters for homeless men, and sued again to shelter homeless women. And sued once more to house homeless families. What kind of leadership leaves the governing of our city to the courts? Common decency, conscience, and commitment compels us to do better.[14]

HOMELESSNESS

If a man or a woman is lying on the street and wants to sleep there tonight, that man or woman has a serious problem. Now, the left-wing advocates would make you think that everyone on the street just needs a place to live, and is something like Saint Francis of Assisi. The right-wing advocates would make you think that everyone lying on the street is some kind of a predatory criminal that wants to harm everyone and hurt everyone. There may be a few people lying on the street in either category. But the truth is that most people lying on the street fall somewhere in between what the advocates for the poverty industry and the right-wingers would have you believe. Most of the people lying on the street have a problem. Their problems vary. They run a spectrum. In most cases, they're much more complex than simply lack of a home.

～

Where does the right to sleep on the streets come from? It doesn't come from anywhere. It isn't in the Constitution of the United States. It certainly isn't a right you would invoke if one of your relatives was sleeping on the streets.

～

HUMOR

A few years ago he couldn't have done that. The mobsters would have stopped him at the fish market.[15]

> —*at the premiere of* Godzilla, *referring to the monster's destructive stroll through the city*

I've never lived here. I've never worked here. I ain't never been here. But I think it would be cool to be your senator.

> —*joking on* The Late Show with David Letterman *about what he would say if he was running for the U.S. Senate in Arkansas, countering Hillary Rodham Clinton's run for the Senate in New York*

We have 412 expressionless statues in Central Park. You have Al Gore.[16]

> —*speaking at a dinner in Washington, D.C., in 1999*

INNOVATION

That's what an innovative, creative society does. It embraces new ideas. It doesn't let all kinds of irrational fears keep us from taking up experiments that have worked elsewhere.

INSPIRATION

The genius of America, the thing that makes this country the greatest country in the history of the world—with all of its flaws and all of its problems—is the idea that you can be anything you want to be if you work hard enough to get there.

~

Problems are challenges to do better.

~

Who can doubt our independent spirit . . . our self-reliance . . . our determination?

~

History is not predestined or preordained. The world of tomorrow is created by the choices we make today . . . choices that reflect the importance of every human being.

~

Does everybody remember Plato? Plato developed the notion of the ideal. You never reached it. But in striving to get there, you kept making improvements in society.[17]

~

Perhaps better than anyone of our time, Dr. (Martin Luther) King knew how difficult it is to change the world. But most of all, he knew that violent change does not result in permanent change.

⁓

Most of what we've accomplished are things that people thought we couldn't do. So there's no reason why we can't do more things that people think cannot be done.

⁓

JUDITH NATHAN

She's been a very good friend to me before I had to deal with the decision that I have to make about my illness and what to do about it, and I rely on her, and she helps me a great deal.[18]

⁓

LIBERTY

All that we have done, all that we must continue to do together, is based on continuing to liberate the human spirit, understanding that liberty is a balance of freedom and responsibility, of rights and obligations.

~

LITTLE LEAGUE BASEBALL

It was an unfortunate and serious mistake made by adults to misrepresent the age of one of the team members. That decision sadly hurts all the dedicated young boys who played their hearts out throughout the season, and postseason play. The city has no intention of asking that the keys to the city be returned. It would only add to the hurt and pain that the innocent children of this team are already experiencing. Hopefully, all those involved will learn a valuable lesson about the importance of honesty and integrity in sports.

—referring to the controversy surrounding the Little League Baseball team from the Bronx that used overaged player Danny Almonte

MONICA LEWINSKY

I'll never mention it, it only made them more popular. Anyway, it's not an issue of mine.[19]

—answering a query in 1999 about what he thought of the subject of Monica Lewinsky and Bill Clinton

PREJUDICE

I believe the best way to combat prejudice is to examine and expose the irrational process that makes someone a bigot.

~

Haters come in all colors, shapes, and sizes. And so do their victims. The haters react to different stimuli . . . their hatred manifests itself in different ways. But all haters go through the same process.

~

So what can elected officials do to promote racial understanding and harmony? We can exercise moral leadership. We can reject appeals to racial, ethnic, and religious division. We can talk and hope that people listen.

~

QUALITY OF LIFE

Quality of life is not so much a destination to be reached as a direction in which to strive. Quality of life is a continuous process. It demands an ongoing effort.

~

All that we have accomplished, all that must be done in the future, rests on a foundation of public safety and improved quality of life.

~

Noise pollution happens to be harder to enforce than other quality of life problems, but we are going to do our best.

~

People's conception of urban America has changed from a place that was derelict, decayed, filled with unemployment and union difficulties, to a much more realistic and positive place that is dedicated to improving the quality of life of its residents.

~

High gas prices in March 2000 inspired Giuliani to seek a repeal of the 1993 federal gas tax increase. He is joined here by Bob Ravallo, a concerned local councilman. (Stuart Ramson, AP/Wide World Photos)

RESPONSIBILITY

We must reinforce the notion that you're not a man if you bring a child into this world and you don't take responsibility for that child.

〜

SECURITY

Man! Look, it's a big city, and you get some real weirdos who hang out in this city, and that's what I was worried about on, uh, New Year's Eve. I wasn't, you know—I figured the terrorist groups and all that we could keep under control—worried, but who knows what, what's living in some cave somewhere.[20]

—during a call-in radio show after going toe to toe with critic John Hynes, a livery cab industry activist

〜

SENATE RACE

I can't discuss what she's for until she says what she's for.[21]

—reacting to a question about what he thought of Hillary Rodham Clinton's stance on issues going into their short-lived Senate race

〜

TWA FLIGHT 800

We share this loss together, not as men or women from different nations or religions or races, but as all children of the same God. Our grief and our sorrow show us that there is strength—great strength—in coming together and sharing what we lost.

In our lifetimes, there are just a handful of moments, occasions that you will always remember where you were and what you were doing when you found out that a tragedy had occurred.

The experience of Flight 800 reminds us all that our true strength, our real strength . . . comes from our families, from our homes, from our churches, our synagogues, our communities. It comes from people relying on each other and helping each other and people being able to count on the support of others.

TERRORISM

We should not be afraid of terrorism. If you let them control your behavior, they win.[23]

—*spoken in 1996, five years before the attacks on the World Trade Center*

VIOLENCE

Cries can't go unanswered. Screams can't go unheard. Bruises can't go unseen. In the year 2000 I want us to realize that the protection, health, and safety of children is the job of all New Yorkers, so that the children of our city can lead more secure lives. But to do that we must also protect them from the crime of domestic violence.

VISION

We've become a city where new ideas are welcomed and actually put to the test. Some of these ideas work better than others—but we are continually thinking and looking for solutions. And that's what matters.

Y2K

When the ball dropped on New Year's Eve, I have to tell you—I was elated and enormously pleased at the tremendous progress that the city has made, and at the fact that New York was the center of everything when the world entered the new millennium. But I also have to admit to you that I was very nervous, and I was afraid. I was afraid that something would go wrong . . . that despite the great planning of the police department, and of emergency personnel, that some terrible thing would happen to harm people or hurt the city.

A Few Final Words as Mayor

I wonder how much of it was bluff. A lot of it had to be bluff. Churchill could not have known England was going to prevail. He hoped it, but there was no way he could know. . . . Look, in a crisis you have to be optimistic. When I said the spirit of the city would be stronger, I didn't know that. I just hoped that. There are parts of you that say, Maybe we're not going to get through this. . . . You don't listen to them.[1]

—referring to Winston Churchill's confidence-inducing public speeches during World War II

RUDY, WAY TO GO! YOU'RE ABOUT THE GREATEST MAYOR EVER, AIN'TCHA?[2]

—New York City ironworker Dwayne Dent, calling out to Giulianiust

People didn't elect me to be a conciliator. If they just wanted a nice guy, they would have stayed with Dinkins. They wanted someone who was going to change this place. How do you expect me to change it if I don't fight with somebody? You don't change ingrained human behavior without confrontation, turmoil, anger.[3]

There's no question that the only reason I was selected (*Time* magazine's) Person of the Year is the people of New York are the people of the year.[4]

I think from the outside, when people look at political officials and political leaders, they think they're walking around with a big plan in their hand. But by and large, you let it happen and make decisions as they come up.[5]

Our city and our nation have never been stronger or more united, and our faith in the strengths of community and humanity has been bolstered by countless stories of heroism and sacrifice.

At an October 2001 news conference, Giuliani announced he would not attempt to buck term limits by seeking a third term as New York City mayor. There had been ample speculation he would try to stay in office beyond his two terms in the wake of the terrorist attacks on the World Trade Center. (Suzanne Plunkett, AP/Wide World Photos)

I don't believe that I've changed. On September 11, 12, 13, I did the same things . . . the same things I've done when we've had fires and catastophes . . . except it was on a different scale.[6]

⌒

This place (Ground Zero) has to be santified. This place has to become a place in which whenever anybody comes here, immediately they're going to feel the great power and strength and emotion of what it means to be an American.[7]

⌒

We're not in a different world. It's the same world as before, except now we understand it better. The threat and danger were there, but now we recognize it. So it's probably a safer world now.[8]

⌒

We have proven to the world that New Yorkers do not back down from challenges. Equipped with this strong momentum and the recognition that fiscal responsibility has been key to our city's economic boom over the past eight years, I know that New York City will overcome any challenges that we may face in the future.

⌒

NOTES

POLITICS AS UNUSUAL

1. *George*, April 1999.
2. Ibid.
3. Rubin, Ron, *Rudy, Rudy, Rudy: The Real and the Rational*. New York: Holmes and Meier, 2000, 15, from *New York Post*, April 8, 1999.
4. *George*, April 1999.
5. Rubin, 51, from *New York Times*, December 30, 1998.
6. *New York Times*, September 28, 2001.
7. *Village Voice*, February 15, 2000.
8. *Economist*, March 22, 1997.
9. Rubin, 3, from *Esquire*, October 1997.
10. Ibid., 24, from *New York Times*, December 3, 1995.
11. Ibid., 75, from *New York Times*, August 18, 1994.
12. Ibid., 119, from *Riverdale Press*, July 18, 1996.
13. Ibid., 142, from *New York Post*, May 3, 2000.
14. Ibid., 170, from *New York Times*, January 23, 2000.
15. Ibid., 170, from *New York Post*, June 11, 1999.
16. Kirtzman, Andrew, *Rudy Giuliani: Emperor of the City*. New York: William Morrow, 2000, 98.
17. Ibid., 195.
18. Ibid., 223.
19. Ibid., 227.

A BITE OUT OF CRIME

1. *New Republic*, January 15, 2001.
2. Rubin, Ron, *Rudy, Rudy, Rudy: The Real and the Rational.* New York: Holmes and Meier, 2000, 7, from *New York Daily Times*, June 9, 1985.
3. Compiled by Robert Lederman, president of A.R.T.I.S.T., from *New York Times*, July 5, 1998.
4. Ibid., from Associated Press, April 30, 1998.
5. *Village Voice*, February 15, 2000.
6. *Newsweek*, April 5, 1999.
7. Rubin, 83, from *New York Daily News*, September 25, 1996.

NEW YORK, NEW YORK

1. Rubin, Ron, *Rudy, Rudy, Rudy: The Real and the Rational.* New York: Holmes and Meier, 2000, 150, from *New York Daily News*, July 26, 1997.
2. Kirtzman, Andrew, *Rudy Giuliani: Emperor of the City.* New York: William Morrow, 2000, 55.

SCHOOLS AND EDUCATION

1. Compiled by Robert Lederman, president of A.R.T.I.S.T., from a Giuliani press release, October 13, 1998.
2. *Village Voice*, February 15, 2000.
3. Rubin, Ron, *Rudy, Rudy, Rudy: The Real and the Rational.* New York: Holmes and Meier, 2000, 101, from *New York Times*, July 25, 1993.
4. Ibid., 185, from *New York Daily News*, February 28, 1997.

NEW YORK'S BRAVEST AND FINEST

1. *New York Times*, September 17, 2001.
2. Ibid.
3. *Newsweek*, April 5, 1999.
4. Rubin, Ron, *Rudy, Rudy, Rudy: The Real and the Rational*. New York: Holmes and Meier, 2000, 79, from *Esquire*, October 1997.

RUDY HIS OWN SELF

1. *George*, April 1999.
2. Ibid., quoting the *Washington Post*.
3. Barrett, Wayne, assisted by Adam Fifield, *Rudy! An Investigative Biography of Rudolph Giuliani*. New York: Basic Books, 2000, 396.
4. *George*, April 1999.
5. *New York Times*, August 1, 2001.
6. Compiled by Robert Lederman, president of A.R.T.I.S.T., from *New York Daily News*, October 25, 1998.
7. Ibid., from *New York Times*, June 24, 1998.
8. Ibid., from *New York Times*, July 22, 1998.
9. Ibid., from *New York Times*, November 13, 1998.
10. Ibid., from *New York Post*, November 13, 1998.
11. *Village Voice*, May 23, 2000.
12. *Time South Pacific*, July 19, 1999.
13. Rubin, Ron, *Rudy, Rudy, Rudy: The Real and the Rational*. New York: Holmes and Meier, 2000, 7, from *New York Daily News*, October 24, 1998.
14. Ibid., 69, from *New York Post*, April 9, 1999.

15. Ibid., 191, from *New York Times*, December 31, 1998.
16. Kirtzman, Andrew, *Rudy Giuliani: Emperor of the City*. New York: William Morrow, 2000, 125.
17. Ibid., 49.
18. Ibid., 138.
19. Ibid., 466.
20. Barrett and Fifield, 285.

SPORTS AND CULTURE

1. Rubin, Ron, *Rudy, Rudy, Rudy: The Real and the Rational*. New York: Holmes and Meier, 2000, 2, from *New York Post*, October 30, 1996.
2. *Village Voice*, February 15, 2000.
3. Kirtzman, Andrew, *Rudy Giuliani: Emperor of the City*. New York: William Morrow, 2000, 264.
4. *Village Voice*, February 15, 2000.

BUSINESS

1. Murdock, Deroy, Scripps Howard News Service, October 12, 2001.

HIS PROSTATE CANCER

1. About.com Poll, May 19, 2000.
2. *Christian Science Monitor*, June 22, 2000.
3. Newsweek Web, September 25, 2001.
4. Rubin, Ron, *Rudy, Rudy, Rudy: The Real and the Rational*. New York: Holmes and Meier, 2000, 177, from *New York Post*, May 20, 2000.
5. *Time*, May 29, 2000.
6. Kirtzman, Andrew, *Rudy Giuliani: Emperor of the City*. New York: William Morrow, 2000, 286.
7. *Village Voice*, May 9, 2000.

SEPTEMBER 11 AND THE AFTERMATH

1. Newsweek Web, September 25, 2001.
2. Murdock, Deroy, Scripps Howard News Service, September 14, 2001.
3. Newsweek Web, September 25, 2001.
4. Ibid.
5. Ibid.
6. *New York Times*, September 14, 2001.
7. Ibid.
8. *New York Times*, September 20, 2001.
9. Newsweek Web, September 25, 2001.
10. Murdock.
11. *New York Times*, September 16, 2001.
12. *New York Times*, September 20, 2001.
13. *New York Times*, October 8, 2001.
14. *Newsweek*, September 24, 2001.

RUDY REDUX

1. *New York Times*, November 12, 2001.
2. *New York Times*, November 13, 2001.
3. Compiled by Robert Lederman, president of A.R.T.I.S.T., from News Radio 88, May 21, 1998.
4. Kirtzman, Andrew, *Rudy Giuliani: Emperor of the City*. New York: William Morrow, 2000, 225.
5. *Newsweek*, April 5, 1999.
6. *Time*, March 16, 1998.
7. Kirtzman, 224.
8. Rubin, Ron, *Rudy, Rudy, Rudy: The Real and the Rational*. New York: Holmes and Meier, 2000, 183, from *New York Post*, March 10, 1998.
9. Kirtzman, 278.

10. Ibid., 280–81.
11. *Christian Science Monitor*, October 31, 1997.
12. *Village Voice*, February 15, 2000.
13. Compiled by Robert Lederman, president of A.R.T.I.S.T., from *New York Newsday*, April 20, 1998.
14. Barrett, Wayne, assisted by Adam Fifield, *Rudy! An Investigative Biography of Rudolph Giuliani*. New York: Basic Books, 2000, 191.
15. *Time Canada*, June 1, 1998.
16. Rubin, 159, from *New York Times*, November 10, 1999.
17. Ibid., 56, from *New York Times*, February 26, 1998.
18. Kirtzman, 281.
19. *Time South Pacific*, July 19, 1999.
20. *Village Voice*, May 23, 2000.
21. *Time South Pacific*, July 19, 1999.
22. Kirtzman, 286.
23. Rubin, 31, from *New York Times*, March 10, 1996.

A FEW FINAL WORDS AS MAYOR

1. *Time*, December 31, 2001–January 7, 2002.
2. Ibid.
3. Ibid.
4. *USA Today*, December 28, 2001.
5. Ibid.
6. Ibid.
7. Ibid.
8. *Time*, December 31, 2001–January 7, 2002.

NEW YORK CITY MAYORAL SPEECHES, WEEKLY COLUMNS, AND PRESS RELEASES SOURCED

First inauguration speech, January 2, 1994.

State of the city address, January 11, 1995.

"A Vision for Education," the Wharton Club, August 11, 1995.

Address before the United Nations General Assembly, September 19, 1995.

Domestic Violence Rally, City Hall, October 2, 1995.

Address on Tolerance, March 26, 1996.

June 3, 1996, press release.

Memorial service for passengers of TWA Flight 800, Smithport Beach, Long Island, July 22, 1996.

Personal Responsibility and Work Opportunity, Reconciliation Act of 1996, September 11, 1996.

September 25, 1996, press release.

Conference on the New Immigrants, Cowles Auditorium, Minneapolis, September 30, 1996.

Kennedy School of Government, Cambridge, Massachusetts, October 10, 1996.

New York Yankees celebration, City Hall, October 29, 1996.

State of the City Address, January 14, 1997.

Citizens Crime Commission speech, March 6, 1997.

Testimony before the House Committee on Government Reform, March 13, 1997.

Smart Schools Announcement, P.S. 66 Richmond Hill, Queens, May 20, 1997.

New York City Conference on Immigration, Ellis Island, June 10, 1997.

TWA Flight 800 Memorial Mass, St. Patrick's Cathedral,
        July 17, 1997.

New Urban Agenda, delivered at Kennedy School of Government,
        September 29, 1997.

"Removing Drugs from Our Neighborhoods and Schools,"
        October 1, 1997.

"Freeing the Economy from Organized Crime and Restoring Open,
        Competitive Markets," October 23, 1997.

Victory Speech, Hilton Grand Ballroom, November 4, 1997.

"The Entrepreneurial City," the Manhattan Institute,
        December 3, 1997.

Second inaugural address, "The Agenda for Permanent Change,"
        January 1, 1998.

The State of the City Address, January 14, 1998.

Martin Luther King, Jr., Birthday Ceremony, Tweed Gallery,
        January 14, 1997.

"The Next Phase of Quality of Life: Creating a More Civil City,"
        February 24, 1998.

Address to the Forum Club: Restoring the Centrality of Work to
        New York City Life, March 25, 1998.

Press release proclaiming May 1, 1998, as Law Day.

"Reaching Out to All New Yorkers by Restoring Work to the
        Center of City Life," Republic National Bank, Manhattan,
        July 20, 1998.

"Rethinking America's Misguided Drug Policies," North Carolina,
        October 22, 1998.

"Strengthening Biomedical Research and Development to Enable
        Innovation, Create Jobs and Prepare our Economy for the
        21st Century," Russ Berrie Pavilion Conference Center,
        Columbia University, December 8, 1998.

Joe DiMaggio's Memorial Service, April 23, 1999.

Reagan Lecture, Ronald Reagan Presidential Library,
September 30, 1999.

State of the City address, January 13, 2000.

"New York Is Off and Running for the 2012 Olympics," Mayor's
Weekly Column, March 27, 2000.

"How New Yorkers Can Help Protect the City from West Nile
Virus," Mayor's Weekly Column, April 3, 2000.

April 27, 2000, press conference.

Remarks to the Conference of Mayors on Restoring Accountability
to City Government, May 9, 2000.

May 15, 2000, press conference.

"Building a Healthier New York for the 21st Century," Mayor's
Weekly Column, June 19, 2000.

"The Boroughs are Booming," Mayor's Weekly Column,
July 10, 2000.

"A Public/Private Partnership Builds School Athletic Fields,"
Mayor's Weekly Column, July 17, 2000.

"New York City Welcomes Record Number of Visitors," Mayor's
Weekly Column, August 14, 2000.

"Bold New Initiatives for a New School Year," Mayor's Weekly
Column, August 28, 2000.

"Leading New York's Finest in a New Century," Mayor's Weekly
Column, September 11, 2000.

"City Mourns Mideast Terror Victims," Mayor's Weekly Column,
October 16, 2000.

"New York is the Baseball Capital of the World," Mayor's Weekly
Column, October 23, 2000.

"New Ideas to Educate Our Children," Mayor's Weekly Column,
December 11, 2000.

Keynote Address to New York City Conference on School Choice,
    December 13, 2000.

"The Second Harlem Renaissance," Mayor's Weekly Column,
    February 26, 2001.

"Beat the Beetles!", Mayor's Weekly Column, March 12, 2001.

"Honoring New York's Bravest," Mayor's Weekly Column,
    July 2, 2001.

Remarks at Naturalization Ceremony on Ellis Island with President
    Bush, July 10, 2001.

"Reaffirming New York's Commitment to Immigration," Mayor's
    Weekly Column, July 16, 2001.

"Building on Our Record of Success in Public Health," Mayor's
    Weekly Column, August 20, 2001.

August 31, 2001, press release concerning decision by Little League
    Baseball to strip titles from Rolando Paulino All-Stars Little
    League team for knowingly using overaged player Danny
    Almonte.

Remarks at the Fire Department Promotions Ceremony,
    September 16, 2001.

Citywide Prayer Service at Yankee Stadium, September 23, 2001.

"Our Darkest Day; Our Finest Hour," Mayor's Weekly Column,
    September 24, 2001.

Address to the United Nations General Assembly on Combatting
    Terrorism, October 1, 2001.

"Responsible Governing Will Lead to Our Recovery," Mayor's
    Weekly Column, October 15, 2001.

"Refusing to Give in to Fear," Mayor's Weekly Column,
    October 22, 2001.

"The Yankees—New York's October Tradition," Mayor's Weekly
        Column, October 29, 2001.
"New York City Is Thriving," Mayor's Weekly Column,
        November 5, 2001.
"Common Bonds Unite and Strengthen Us Once Again," Mayor's
        Weekly Column, November 19, 2001.
"Continuing Business Development and Job Creation Citywide,"
        Mayor's Weekly Column, December 3, 2001.
"Countering Budget Gaps with Budgetary Discipline," Mayor's
        Weekly Column, December 10, 2001.